Taproots

❧

Taproots

Where Ideas Are Born

CAROL EGMONT ST. JOHN

Twin Lights Publishers, Inc.

Rockport, Massachusetts

TAPROOTS: WHERE IDEAS ARE BORN

Cover design, typography, and page layout
Sharp Des!gns, Inc., Lansing, MI

Front cover: *Where Lilies Bloom* (Oil, 11 × 14)
Back cover: *Emerging Woman* (Watercolor, 28 × 35)

ISBN 1-885435-04-5

Printed in China

Contents

Acknowledgments

To write and paint without an audience is one thing. To find support and appreciation is another. I wish to thank all the art patrons who complimented my work by buying it; my fellow artist-writer friends who fed me with their own rich art spirits, and my dear friend, Joan Frank, who read and critiqued every word in this book.

I am also forever indebted to the mentorship of Carole Wood Hardy, a fellow poet who encouraged my poetry; my mother, who fostered my imagination; my thesis advisor, Glenda Bissex, who years ago encouraged me to look at the relationship between art and writing; editor Glenda Martin, who was the first to read and affirm *Taproots;* and Dr. Doris Hunter, who nurtured my public voice and convinced me I had something to say. Most of all, I must thank Doris Patey who believed in the veracity and importance of this compilation of work and made its publication possible.

Please note that these acknowledgements are all directed to women; women helping women; women like me. I have learned through them the power in each of us to inspire and empower one another.

Emerging Woman (Watercolor, 28 × 35)

Preface

Taproots is a compilation of writing and artwork representing a twenty-five-year exploration. It was during a year-long retrospective study of my own process and products that I began to see where my paintings and poetry were sourced. In this book, I have chosen poems, paintings, and homilies, and arranged them not by history, but as examples of the way one artist drew from her personal wellspring. In both my poetry and art I inadvertently reveal unspoken beliefs, take risks, and make inroads to my subconscious. This is the journey of the artistic spirit.

I am coming from three perspectives: one as a writer, another as an artist, and a third as teacher. Working in these disciplines has taught me that the relationship of art to writing and writing to art results in the enrichment of both. The following pages are a look at words and images that are related to one another (some overtly, others by chance) in metaphoric language.

Sprinkled throughout the book are pep talks to get you started and keep you going, ways to source your material, and some heuristics you might try for experimental work of your own. I am hoping to inspire you to seek the revelatory experience of going to your well and finding it full.

Metaphors

Burning the Midnight Oil (Oil, 20 × 16)

Metaphors

Think allegories, parables, fables, and caterpillars. Each represents ideas beyond the literal. So too, the languages of the poet, the painter, and the dreamer. They speak to us in figurative comparisons we call metaphors. Often we think we are writing about one thing but it turns out we are expressing another. When an unexpected metaphor shows up, this is the thrill of it all.

The same thing can be true about a piece of art. We have our tools, an idea—and we begin, but often the motivation behind our subject matter is more profound than we initially understood. In a good painting something moves us, and that something falls into the meaning we bring to the image.

I once thought painting was a way to talk about subjects that went beyond language, and the poem was language stretching itself to the loftiest use of words. Later, I discovered they are simply two invented languages; one reinforcing the other.

My metaphors reoccur in both my poetry and painting. They may be revealed in a dark passage, a slant of light, a heavy line, or a lost one. They may be found in the subject matter, the design, or the colors. Much like the dream brings one's deep consciousness to the surface, the poem and the painting pull from the same well and are profoundly personal—ergo, enlightening.

The poem "Widow Mother" is about my parents and their shared love of books. The painting *Burning the Midnight Oil* describes my inherited involvement with the written word.

In the pages that follow, using a sampling of paintings and poems, I will attempt to illustrate the role of metaphor in the creative process.

Setting the Stage

To begin, she needs an attic
One with musty floor boards that creak
A trunk alive with memories
Cast-off clothes, an abacus

She must be silent, burrow, go
So far inside that climbing out
Makes all the difference.
No Prozac, Valium or Zanex,
No aspirin, even, allowed.

Pain has its place right next to joy.
She may find those baby pictures—
The one of her Dad's arms
Lifting his platinum trophy
Wisps of hair laughing at sunshine
Pink dots for toes, blithely safe.

These memories are as welcome
As the blue garter of a teenage bride
Who planned her young wedding
Wanting a world she'd learned from Hollywood
The one with the happy ending.

Let the journals be found
That tell the rest of the story
Of lust born at thirty and the
Cosmic kickball that sent her spinning
Through space 'til she fell into an abyss
So deep she forgot sky.

Be sure there is a window
Where she can see rusting rocks against blue sea
The black and white clarity of a merganzer
The play of an eider.

Ah—yes—now the poem can begin.

The Book (Oil, 16 × 20)

Widow Mother

I was only seven
when my father died
she collapsed on his coffin
and begged him not to go
I could not watch
and do not know who
stood her on her feet.

Silence sealed our house
for months that stretched
like Winter Harbor fog
its mist, wetter than rain

until she remembered
and became *responsible*
removed their leather-bound
books of Shelley and Keats
from the high book shelves

his notations in the margins
(tall pointy strokes)
and her poems to him
(simple soft profound)
among the gilded pages

She buried them in the cellar
in cardboard boxes marked
CONSUMABLE
where they grew moldy
wept and turned to dust

Then cut her long braid
and placed it in a drawer
beneath some flowered silk
bought tailored suits
and gave her dreams to me.

The Reader (Watercolor, 16 × 20)

The Right to Write

All the past up to a moment ago is your legacy. You have a right to it. The work of ancient masters, those of the student next to you, the remark let drop a moment ago: all is experience. . . ."

—Robert Henri, *The Art Spirit*

You are a part of a bigger picture, unique unto that picture and essential to its wholeness. Everything that has happened before you has led to this moment. It is both a universal moment and yours alone. If you can subscribe to this, you can subscribe to the theory that you have something to say.

Too many of us doubt ourselves. Teaching a writing class for teachers one year, I asked participants to talk about their relationship to writing. One woman said simply, "I am not creative." I knew, of course, she was, but I hoped the week ahead would substantiate more than encouraging platitudes. When we began to write, the woman's eyes rolled back in her head and she fainted.

Extreme? I guess so, but how many of us doubt the well inside, and fear we are blockheads who cannot get to the source? We are not empty. Indeed, we are profound!

We have the stardust of millenniums coursing through our veins; each of us beginning life with the sweetness of innocence and the natural instincts of primitive discovery. Our first accidental sounds and scratches evolve into symbols that have taken a mere twenty thousand years to assemble. Are we not remarkable to advance our skills the distance of all history in only five to ten years? Is it not even more remarkable that each of us has something to contribute to the bank?

The Evolving Self (Watercolor, 16 × 20)

Permission to Paint

Just look at the details, my father would say. *She has her mother's eye.*
—Westy Egmont (author's father)

Some of us were blessed with families or teachers who encouraged and integrated art into our childhood, insuring us of ready access to that energy. Many of us were less fortunate.

Myself, I was ordained to be an artist. From the beginning, my drawings were saved; crazy little people with spiked hair, stick bodies, massive hands, and pupils dilated in round, frightened eyes.

"Carol: age 2."

"Carol: age 2 and 6 months."

I drew on walls, tables, books, and pads. The punishments varied. I still cannot leave a pen or pencil alone. My phone book is a disaster.

My doodles ultimately became a resource for my current painting style. They are the purest expression of me. The primal me before education taught me all the rules.

We are all artists. Some of us have had advantages, but it is never too late to claim what is rightfully ours. Viewing the art of interned criminals, seeing paintings rendered by a paraplegic and those of a blind man, or the art created within the walls of a death camp like Terezan, is overwhelming evidence of the art spirit and our human need to record and express ourselves graphically.

Child's drawing (Crayon, 8½ × 11)

Jump In!

I enter the icy-cold water off Cape Ann in midsummer. It is hot, I want to get wet, the ocean teases me with its promise of exhiliration, but I stand with the waves lapping at my toes. My toes shiver. I have two clear choices ahead: I can immerse myself bit by bit, wincing each time the ocean swallows up another inch or two of my hot body, or I can shallow-dive into the waves, all at once, glide through the deep green coldness, feel my hot blood jolt with its sudden change in temperature, and come up for air gloriously, shaking water from my hair, and thrilled. Once I am completely wet, the ocean and I are on equal terms. Until then, I am timid; it is vast and threatening.

The ocean is your blank paper or canvas! How easily it intimidates, mocks, induces paralysis of the paintbrush. One thing is certain: you're staring at it because you want to get into it. On timid days you may begin tentatively. A sketch, perhaps, a testing of color on the palette, a few small touches to the paper. The dance is questioning, searching, but it is a beginning. In another mood, diving into that paper is the way to fulfillment.

Exercise

Take your largest brush, mix up a color and splash it across the surface. There! It is shivery, but the ball is in your court now. The color asks for something else. You know what it wants. Try a new mix, or a pure hue, dab it on, and now there are the three of you, beginning a dance, a swimmy, pulling and pushing and dripping dance. The wetter you get, the less you tremble, the more you are immersed.

With your wet brush draw a shape or shapes into your color. Let it run and become itself. Study its light and texture, its surprises, and leave it like a signature with no more needed to be said.

The Red Tide (Tempera on kraft paper, 12 × 16)

Talent

The myth of talent gets in our way. Don't believe it. To be creative is to be human. Can you talk? Do you listen, watch and read? Are you paying attention? If so, you can write. Writing is simply a transference of ideas and observations onto a page. We are scripting all the time.

When we get up in the morning the play begins. What shall we wear? What must we achieve today? Have for breakfast? Not forget?

Even our lists are scripts. Your grocery list is like a poem of your favorite things and of modern life. Imagine Martha Washington reading your shopping list? It would read like science fiction. Tampons, Phisohex, Comet, lactose-free milk, kiwis, bagels.

One way to start to write is to take the basic tools of writing and the most basic structure of words and watch what happens. Start with a word you like. Make a list. Let one word stimulate another by free association. When you are done see if you can find a metaphor.

Lavender . . . Grandma . . . brooch . . . antique . . . Table . . .
plateau . . . mesa . . . Arizona . . . dry . . .

Grandma

The brooch
carved by Danish hands
and as old as a Viking ship
is touched by
her freckled finger
now paler than the moon. Its
lavender lines visit
the young maid's ivory profile
making sure
she is still there.

Read your list aloud. Play with it. Let it please you. Name it.

The Lists (Watercolor, 14 × 18)

Mistakes

Art must include risk or it is not art. Without mistakes, how can we provide ourselves with stepping-stones to growth; to understanding? For too many, the act of taking on a creative endeavor seems to be synonymous with declaring to the whole world, "I shall make no mistakes on this one." If this is your thinking, the inevitable mistakes that follow will be humiliating.

This morning I picked up a seagull quill, one of nature's gifts I use to avoid the predictability of manufactured pens. My intention was to create a large painting from a small doodle I had sketched, but the pen spat—oops! A splattered mistake! I had to reinvent my design. Regarding the ink as a spontaneous sprinkle of energy, I danced my colors through its rain. The result is bold and fresh. I call it *Night Line*. You can see it on the facing page.

Sometimes mistakes seem unredeemable but it is fun to analyze and manipulate them. They can take you in a new direction. Good and bad should be viewed with equal value, not to the patron, but to the artist who is the eternal student. We are inventors, after all; always experimenting.

Remember Pasteur? Pasteur was not disgusted when mold interrupted his study of tartrate. He didn't pour his soiled solution down the drain, calling it a failure. Instead, he began to observe what the mold did. He took it further into experimental studies leading to the process of fermentation which led to his discoveries about vaccines. Many of us grew to adulthood because of Pasteur's *mistake*.

Exercise

Re-create a rejected painting or piece of writing.

Night Line (Watercolor, 14 × 18)

The Writing Group

Most writers need an audience. Our words need to be spoken so we can hear them and test them. When we get a reaction we can decide if its the one we wanted. It is interesting how, even when only positive comments are made, we can learn from what is said and what isn't said.

Without an audience, it is hard to declare ourselves fit to write. Here, children have an advantage. They tend to think all things are possible if you tell them they are. We adults have to undo a history of red marks and editing tyrants. It's no wonder we must use exercises of self-affirmation.

In my writing group there is a woman who writes in a waterfall of energy. The things she writes causes gasps of wonder because, without affectation or apparent self-consciousness, she unravels truth week after week. We have admonished her for not sending her work out or rewriting it for publication, but she laughs at us and says, "But it's so ordinary."

Like so many of us, she has yet to own her brilliance even with her writing group's support. We are too used to ourselves to know we have voices that can tell stories to enlighten others.

Exercise

Admit it. Admit it again and again. Say it in front of people. Sing it to yourself in the shower! I am a writer. I am a writer! I have something worth saying.

Invite fellow would be/could be writers into your circle. Create a safe harbor by writing together and then before reading your work aloud, establish rules for response. It's magical. As you become each other's mentors, your writing will improve.

The Poet's Circle (Gouache, 36 × 28)

Art and Beholders

We may not believe we are creating art unless we study the art of the world. The elegance and power of primitive shapes could be lost to us; the challenge of the abstract or the triumph of *tromp l'oeil*. You may create something out of pure instinct and not recognize its resemblance to the Fauvists, the Cubists, or some other school of art. Here, knowledge enables. It is good to browse through art history books and see what others call art. Ultimately, it is up to you to decide.

The question *what is art?* has plagued the thinking world throughout recorded history. For the Romans and the Greeks it took on standards of perfection in the human form. For the great tribal nations of Africa, it represented the spirit world and its mysteries. In Hindu culture, art is relegated to the world of mandalas in the form of patterns that encircle and embrace the soul. In Islam, figurative art is considered idolatry so they turn to mosaic abstractions of great complexity.

Where we are, who we are, what we worship, and what we know determines how we see art forms. You are a part of an unending revelation. Your art is as real as your voice, your walk, your dreams, and your prayers. It is a mirror of who you are and a pathway to knowing.

Exercise

Remember your first box of crayons, the one that still had all its points? Using new crayons, draw a picture of your family like you did in kindergarten. Think as you did at six. Look at your picture and love it. No one would say to a child, "No, no it's not right!" At least no one like you. Now, write about your drawing and how it felt to draw. Remembering your child, write about the family you described in your family portrait.

Family Night (Watercolor, 32 × 36)

-Women Dancing the Moon and Stars (Oil, 16 × 20)

Celebrating the Elements
Line • Color • Pattern • Composition

Meaning of a Line

I am a graphologist, a proverbial student and teacher of handwriting analysis. There is little doubt in my mind that no matter how carefully we have been schooled, we express our individuality through our penmanship from the time we become fluid with a pencil. How hard we press, the softness of our curves, the size of our letters, whether they are open or closed—all these things, and hundreds of others, provide insights to the writer.

I have heard artists exclaim when they are studying a painting, *It's all in the slant!* They mean that a strong diagonal line will direct the eye and add a dynamic motion to what may have otherwise been static. Interestingly enough, the slant of your handwriting is important as well. It reveals your nature, your tendency to go away from yourself or to go inward, or simply let your mind dictate your heart.

Don't dwell too much on your lines. Better to paint or draw and then reflect. If you are intending to express one idea and discover you are saying something else, ask yourself what and why. Van Gogh's last paintings of the crows flying over hayfields has such a quiet to them. They are almost ominous in their heavy, horizontal planes. The crows fly laterally along the edge of the horizon like his lost ability to lift himself out of the bottoms. I doubt he planned it that way. I believe his metaphor was un-selfconscious and, therefore, all the more powerful.

Exercise

Do some conscious manipulation of line. Draw a happy line and turn it into something. Make a sad line and see where it takes you. Go on. Play with lonely lines and dense lines. Try anger and confusion. Can you see for yourself how these lines begin to work for you and say what you want to say?

The Swimmers (Crayon and watercolor. 11 × 15)

Borrowing a Line

All stories begin somewhere. Our own magic will take us into unique valleys of thought even when we borrow another's line of verse to start the process. This may seem unethical, but I suggest you allow yourself to be led—only momentarily, of course—and see where you end up. You can give up the borrowed *lead-in* line once you've found your own.

- "Once upon a time . . ." (A fairy tale, Hans Christian Anderson)
- "In this house . . ." (*Solstice Poem*, Margaret Atwood)
- "This is how death came . . ." (*Testimony*, Jane Flanders)
- "I wasn't there when . . ." (*Grandmother*, Marilyn Krysl)
- "I was only seven . . ." (*Teaching America*, Carol E. St. John)
- "I have been thinking about living . . ." (*Lilies*, Mary Oliver))
- "But haven't we always known . . . ?" (*Scientists Find Universe Awash in Tiny Diamonds*, Pat Mayne Ellis)

A poem by Pat Mayne Ellis gave me the line, "*We are awash in creation spumed with diamonds shot through with beauty that survived the deaths of stars.*" I am indebted to the poet for inspiration for the poem on the next page.

Moonshine (Watercolor, 12 × 8)

Writing Class

they play with magic,
searching in reflected light
from yesterday, today,
and more tomorrow.
fired minds conjure gems
so hot they'd forge steel.
the spirits of star children flow
across inner and outer landscapes
remembering who they were, and
discovering who they have become.

silence echoes in pencils
scratching out a banquet,
a mental, emotional feast
held up by truth.
how strong the lines that tuck us in
and at the same time invite us
to go bungee jumping.
we are flying!
fly and spring back   fly and spring back.

And soon there will be
brilliance revealed
dust, older than Jesus, dust
that survived millenniums,
diamonds sown in their very blood

On Color

Color talks. It is manipulative. It can be used in healing; to wake people up and to make another color sing. Place complementary colors (opposites on the color wheel) side by side and watch them vibrate. Orange next to blue, yellow to purple, red to green. A dash of one will exaggerate the other.

Last Glow

Purple pulls gold through
her sultry tones
and lets the rock lavish in twilight.
Ignited edges of trees burn
next to violet silhouettes.

And in the darkest edges,
survivors of the water's beating
and the blistering July sun,
the wild aster triumphs
in her lavender gown.

My long shadow stretches before me
and it is purple, too,
bigger, more oblique, more attached
to the earth than I.

My deepest purples lie within,
those dark channels of my spirit
that make bright days brighter
but hold secrets and pain.

They lie in the creases between my breasts,
the vertical lines between my brows,
the caverns of my person,
in the veins climbing to the surface
of what was once my golden hide.

Complementary Colors (Gouache and acrylic, 18 × 26)

Composition

Composition is one of those elements that a lot of teachers like to teach because there are rules. In writing, it looks like the five-sentence paragraph with an umbrella sentence to start and a summation to close. Neat and predictable, yes, but creative? No guarantees. The average writer is protected by such constructs, but the blithe spirit may be daunted.

In painting, rules for composition come in terms like the *golden mean,* and tricks like placing darkest darks against lightest lights. Then there are those rules of perspective and the frustrations experienced when worrying about vanishing points. Edges of paintings can be as important as centers, and we want to keep the eye entertained with a variety of shapes and sizes.

Colors ask to be meted out thoughtfully, too. There are formulas for the appearance of colors. One artist I know will never use more than three colors on his palette. A warm (yellows, oranges, and reds), a cool (greens and blues), and white. Myself, I like a rainbow on my palette.

Somewhere, I learned about letters and design. The result is that I actually think *S*s, crooked *H*s, *A*s, and *T*s as I lay out compositions. I still have to check my inclination towards dividing a landscape in half with the horizon line or placing my subject matter dead center. In the next painting, can you see the letter *H* in my design? Do you see a pattern of dark and light? Is there a foreground a middle ground and background? It's no accident.

God's Girls (Watercolor, 12 × 9)

Mother's Lesson

She told me God's real name was Truth
And churches were only human
She said everything has purpose
But, you must find it for yourself.

And so I know her death
Demands my life
Her quiet, my voice
Her wisdom, my humility
And losing love
Makes love more dear

Patterns

Remember the Rockettes? It was not just their extraordinary highstepping that packed the Radio City Music Hall, but the patterns and syncronicity of their lines that won our hearts. In music, the repetition of melodies helps us remember them as we hum, tap, or sing along.

In story and art it is the same thing. Chicken Little heard that the sky was falling down—a lot! Andy Warhol let us see as many prints of Marilyn Monroe as we could possibly digest. Jackson Pollack splished and splashed in a spontaneous repetition of style. Matisse made use of patterns, too. He decorated his canvas with the designs of rugs and wallpapers, dresses and screens.

Established patterns help the poet. Constructing couplets, cinquains, Haiku, sonnets, and so on, the writer leans on the familiar to create. Sometimes using a lead-in phrase over and over is an effective way to build a poem.

The pattern in the following poem is created by using prepositions at the beginning of each line.

Heron

as morning breaks, the heron flies
in the near horizon,
atop the marsh
at the fog's edge
through soft green mist
with its great beak leading
from the weighted bank lifting
across cattails and sea grass
over and under its wings sway
between earth and eternity

More Is Less (Tempera, 16 × 12)

The Baby Brigade (Watercolor, 33 × 24)

Openings

Openings
Spotlighted clearings
In summer woods
Meant for studying sky

Openings
Nostrils to tempt
Mouth to satisfy
Pores to learn by osmosis

Openings
Auricles to resonate
Arteries to channel
Pulsating tunnels and caves

Openings
First nights, galas
Receptions, premieres,
Motivations to start again

Openings
Rays through dark clouds
April's crocus
The monarch's first stretch

Exercise

Begin each verse with *Follow me!*

The Vermont Road (Watercolor, 24 × 16)

The Gardener (Watercolor and gouache, 35 × 28)

Foraging for Metaphors

⤫

Foraging for Metaphors

Metaphors show up. You don't have to go hunting for them, all you have to do is notice. Take for example, the book. After I observed that books appear in a number of my paintings and poems, I asked myself *why?* What personal metaphor does the book express?

If I was a scholar, it might be learning. If I was from a Bible-centered home, it might be truth. Being neither of these things, I realize books represent intimate experiences for me. It's a time where my mind opens and is willing to look inside another's.

Exercise

For fun, look at your own metaphors.

1. You are a book. Who reads you? Describe your cover. Are you fiction or nonfiction? Who are your leading characters? Are you beach material or required reading?

2. If you were a boat, how many people could board you? How would you be locomoted? What are your lines and your colors? How well do you handle?

3. If you were a tree, what kind of tree would you be? Gather data about its nature. With what qualities can you identify? Draw or describe your tree by focusing on details. Do a pencil rubbing of its bark. Study its seed, a leaf, a twig. Trust me: you will find a deeper relationship with this tree than you ever thought possible.

Divine Evidence

Common mollusk
swirl of bone white, spun calcium,
freckled as my own sun stained hands,
fractal of the sea's edge,
you are the source of jade handled fans,
of pleats and plates and pillboxes.

Don't ask me to believe
an unconscious architect
designed your fluted hem, or
the sinuous striations tied fast
at your knotty hinge.
Molded seafoam, carved by ancient instincts,
You are too profound in your deliverance
To be labeled *common!*

I shall fill you with rose petals
And place you on my winter windowsill.

Flotsam and Jetsam (Watercolor, 18 × 14)

Arachnid Power

I am the mother
The source who
Drops her drag line
Of sheer liquid crystal
Stretches and sways
To tangle strands
Of silk,
Transparent steel,
So strong,
Only God or
A blue heat could
Melt them down

And you are my child.

The Web (Watercolor, 12 × 16)

Apples for the Teacher

The sprites arrive, their skin lit by innocence.
Bouncing bubbles of hot pinks and blues and greens;
No wall or roof can stop them.
They tumble in, grazing tables and chairs.

Each brings an unwrappable gift.
A boy's recorder toots *Hot Cross Buns*.
Christmas is danced by a sugar plum fairy
In a polo shirt and too-short tights.

After small fingers stretch across black and white keys,
Comes a drawing of a dead dog lying in a colored pencil heaven.
Then an imitation of Elvis snorting *Jingle Bell Rock*.

It is during the applause and thanks a small voice asks,
"What about me? I have brought you a gift, too."
She looks away, to tangled grays
In a cold mist beyond the window, and
A curious silence stills the class.

When she turns, her eyes have sent silver
Rivulets cascading down her cheeks.
Smiling in her own rain, she says,
"You see, I have brought you my tears!"

American Pie (Watercolor, 16 × 20)

Marital Art

What is a marriage?
Is it the softness of sagebrush green
Rooted deeply and deceptively strong?
Or are its layers like the striations of
one canyon wall leaning
into another
forever changing?

Perhaps it is just an accidental journey
across unexpected terrain,
stretching itself into sunsets and
hoping to find water on the way.

The Long Terrain (Watercolor, 12 × 16)

45

Abundance

Have it; have it all:
The drenched cormorant spreading her wings
Sunflower seeds spilling for a catbird's feast
Clouds of monarchs converging on Eastern Point.

Have it; have it all:
My fertile self, pregnant, basking in
Anne Tyler's words, as I embrace
The daring of Picasso, the sentiment of Rockwell,
Testing wings too long folded,
Once too timid to soar.

Have it; have it all:
The diapers behind,
The masks put away,
Days less tangled, with
Time stretched for weaving,
For play and performance,
Risk and revelation.

Have it; have it all:
Early mornings in a kitchen
Where French roast coffee
Fills a blue cup; in a studio where
Flowers bloom and landscapes of characters
Are framed in my own perception.

Radiant Harvest (Acrylic, 24 × 30)

Twin Lights (Watercolor, 12 × 16)

The Power of Place

ᘒ

Rocky Neck (Watercolor, 18 × 14)

Tubac Morning (Watercolor, 16 × 12)

The Power of Place

Everywhere is the center of the world.

—Black Elk

Soho; London; Greenwich Village, New York; the Left Bank of Paris, France; Taos, New Mexico; Eureka Springs, Arkansas; and Tubac, Arizona are only a smattering of western Meccas for artists to gather and work. Large and small, they exist because they provide creative alignments and support among those who seek the edges of society. Where you find yourself will affect your work.

Artists have eyes for the world. How they express the world identifies it to itself. Their work is a metaphor for their time in history and the place and culture in which they find themselves. But, that is not easy if one is stuck in the center of the culture. From dead center it is hard to get perspective. It is like marching in the center of a parade and having little awareness of what is going on at the head or tail. The artist needs to be willing to step outside, look from a different vantage point, live among others who will appreciate uniqueness and encourage it.

Art colonies are temporary solutions for those who want to identify with like-minded people. There are travel workshops and schools providing shelter and an expanse of time and space in which to plop yourself for awhile. They offer an immersion in being an artist; thinking, observing, eating, seeing, and sharing with artists.

Workshops are listed on the Internet and in the spring editions of artists' magazines. They can take you to just about any part of the world in which you would like to be.

Whadevahappenta Brooklyn?

hey, whatevahappenta Brooklyn?
Bonamo's Turkish Taffy?
the Carlton Theater, and
swims at the St. George Hotel?
sugar cubes for sweet sixteen
and dancin' to seventy-eights?

or howabout
the junk that was made in Japan?
where's my charm bracelet
my poodle skirt, the Brooklyn Eagle?
or my old ice box?
Does anyone still chug beer at Breezy Point?

didgaevathink
what it used to mean to be
pinned at Brooklyn College
or who was left with their blue
stamp books half full?
how the Dodgers coulda left?

remembada
clothesline lace?
milkmen and breadman?
goin' downtown?
but where did it go?
Loeser's, A&S's and Mays?

Couldgaevaforget
Garfield's pastrami on rye?
Mario's grocery who delivered?
Manny's candy store?
Dr. Bomson's housecalls?

Whaddabout
the song of the trolley?
maypoles in Prospect Park?
the Esplanade on rollerskates?
Nathan's hot dogs in Coney Island?

The day the bums won the series—
it sure was good

Whadevahappenta the party?

Tenement Lace (Watercolor, 24 × 30)

Women Becoming Themselves (Oil, 16 × 20)

Women Who Paint by the Sea

Wharf women are hot
They don't mince words
Or wince at pure alizarin
Spilling like blood from
The heart of their canvases
They hear in color
Dance in strokes
Weep turpentine tears of
Sea salt and pthalo blue
They stand guard against
The pedestrian and
Long for new dimensions
Swearing to make a wave
Not to get lost in the undertow.

Autumn at Oakes Cove

Rusted rocks lean into outcroppings of
brazen oak, whose prehensile fingers
penetrate a cobalt sky.
Hidden is the Copper Paint Factory—
Our Lady of Good Voyage's blue domes.

On a tack from beach to harbor to shore,
The eye is channeled
Above bobbing buoys and lobster pots,
Beyond the orange marker that
warns of rock under tide.

Horns hail the parade of trawlers,
The *Phyllis A.*, *Teresa Marie*, and *Caterina G.*
They wend their way past the barge, the tug,
the oarsman, while still as a tidal pool,
a slender heron watches,
one foot balanced delicately on periwinkles,
smooth chards of glass, an ancient sewer pipe.

The callous chorus of crows endlessly mock
seabirds and seamen beyond the safety of the shore.
They may drown out the last tour boat's mike,
the luffing of an amateur sail, the laughing gull's cry, but to
no avail, the sea's friends are tough and survival is their art.

The Lighthouse (Tempera, 16 × 26)

Mother and Daughter as One

Through sage brush and ironwood
Prickly pear and saguaro
They clamored for the highest
Stone, a throne aloft
On an ancient sea

A place more fit for bobcats
Than catfish
Rattlesnakes than females

They smelled the air
Dry as the riverbed
Dryer than the tears of the
Anasazi

Dryer than the lids
Of the woman they had left
Below
Dry as
The dust of time.

They let a hawk's wing
Clatter towards the horizon
And knew
They were eternal
Children together
On yet a greater plain.

Vantage Point (Oil, 20 × 24)

Sculpture Garden (Watercolor, 26 × 18)

Airport Reception (Watercolor, 24 × 16)

Life as Story

❦

Mother and Child (Watercolor, 18 × 24)

Your Life as a Story

Your life is a story. It is shared by many others, but only you have your perspective and can describe it as it was for you. Indulge yourself in nostalgia. Take a year in your life and try to remember where you were and what happened, or look at the whole timeline of your life! Riffle through the pages of the family album.

When you cast out your line there's no telling what you'll hook! If it's a birthday party, who was there? Who wasn't? Where was it held? Find tiny details to capture even a small slice of the moment. Remember, if you catch a tiger by the tail, you'll be amazed at what it may teach you later.

The Catalyst

I was conceived in passion and
Proud my whole life of it.
I knew from the time I could
Decipher the dates between
A wedding and a birth.
Found the truth in an album,
In white ink on a black field.
The September bride, Louise,
Wore a plain suit and a magnolia corsage.
Only a turn of the page and
April's mother showed her prize.
It is fine to be a love child.
Loved so well by lovers
Their love went legal.

Artifacts

Elsie was my doll, discovered
in the summer house.
I loved her from the minute I saw
her naked foot under the cellar stair.
After I brushed off ancient dust
and tried to open her closed eye,
she endured my endless versions
of *The Ugly Duckling,*
dresses made of rags, dishwater baths
and let me love her fiercely
as I practiced motherhood.

My mother's portrait shows
a girl younger than she ever was for me.
She looks like someone else
someone who had not yet learned
how to answer questions with
questions, read the best parts twice,
someone who knew Georgia O'Keefe's dreams
perhaps George Elliott's.

Here's the heavy silver link bracelet
my grandmother wore
on her freckled Danish wrists.
I remember her faded red hair
piled loosely on her head
the dark blue and purple
dresses above shoes that laced
chicken fricassee Sundays
when *her* mother's language spoke
secrets my ears would never hear.
Little did I know then that time is but a ribbon.

Remembering Raggedy Ann (Watercolor, 14 × 18)

Nicaragua

Terra cotta limbs
lean on my shoulders,
press on my thighs.
Eyes the size
of tidepools
melt the
fears that built
my walls.

I use the language
of the palette
to celebrate.
In verde, azule,
roho and amarillo,
we paint the world
as we want it
to be—
a world with
rainbow ponies
and flowers
like the children
themselves;
bouquets
of beauty unfolding.

The Red Plate (Watercolor, 16 × 12)

The Street Painter

Balanced carefully,
Brow shaded by weathered hat,
Canvas stretched like
An old friend
Welcoming new visions,
The painter seeks
A miracle.

Plein Air Painter (Watercolor, 12 × 16)

Best Friends

a glass of wine
and thee
and talk of misery
of joy
of endings and
beginnings
shifting paradigms
transparent dreams
of schemes
the hole that gnaws
the whole that draws
reaching for wisdom
so we don't get lost
in words about
the weather.

Les Confidentes (Oil, 16 × 20)

Make Way for Poets

Ring your bells for the poets
Let them paint the world in veils of brilliant color.
Put mist in a wintry morning, and
They will summon the sun with a stretch.
If you should lay a shaggy green rug beneath their feet,
Their toes will wiggle the world awake.
Don't show them the columbine or cosmos, no,
They will climb inside and stalk the stamin.
Give them a clumsy chunk of clay instead.
Marvel as they mold it into metaphors.
Tell them an ancient myth,
Then listen to *their* stories of truth.

Should you feed them ripened melon
They will feed *you* a palette of words.
And—
When you inform them you are only human—
They will show you, you're divine.

Dockside Dancin' (Watercolor, 12 × 18)

Night Walk

Over the granite wall she peered,
Beyond the arrows of nasty bushes to
Blue lit parallel profiles
Framed in antique window sash.
She saw their faces, close to bone,
Bodies at right angles in
Uncushioned oak chairs.

Was she playing a ghostly game with
The aging brothers called "The Boys"?
One could hear and the other see.
Order determined their survival. Neighbors
Kept time by their appearance each morning.
Always ties and crisp shirts, long coats in winter.
They dined at Jack's Place seven days a week.

Once there was a wife. But she fell off the porch,
Leaving a quiet bluer than their faces—
Not that there had ever been a noise.
No vacuum sounded, or wash flapped on a line.
No food had ever sizzled on any stove.
Even when she slipped over the railing
She floated silently,
Her neck a mere twig left broken on the ground.

Tuned In (Oil, 16 × 20)

Cock Sure (Oil, 16 × 20)

Humor

Humor

But aren't we really funny? If we couldn't laugh at ourselves and each other how drear it all would be! Humor puts things in a new light. Humor relieves. Humor adds a light touch to a dark space. Humor wants us to befriend it and notice how close it is to tragedy, to vulnerability.

Allow yourself the privilege of taking on the people you love/hate in your life. They will spark your imagination. Exaggerate them, point out their shortcomings, forgive them with a laugh and a shrug, or get beyond the funny to the pathos of their human frailty. Whatever you do, don't ignore them. They are the color, the drama, and the challenge. In them you will find your own story and no doubt the story of others.

Experiment

For fun, think of someone you consider to be an interesting person in his or her surroundings. Imagine their stuff: a desk, a vehicle, a closet or a car, maybe a handbag, and see if you can conjure up enough to write a telling portrait.

Or write a description of what is under your daughter's bed, perhaps living in *your* refrigerator. Context provides such insight to personality.

Pick up your brush and begin with a point of view. Focus not on the truth but the thing that will most clearly support your prejudice. Have fun.

The painting, *The Balancing Act*, is my portrait of a person who is always at risk; the construct of his life out of control. Struggling to have it all, he teeters precariously between two places, his neck stretched out and his support systems meager.

The Balancing Act (Watercolor and gouache, 26 × 35)

The Visionary

He saw beyond the window frame, the rooftops, and the meadow,
He leaned into the clouds and worked to Christianize the ghetto.

I stood behind and listened to the kettle's wild wail,
I washed his clothes, swept the floor and read the morning's mail.

He spoke of the Sophists, pedagogy and didactics
Went from Kant to Kierkegaard and then to the monastics.

I bought the bread and wine, cleaned the toilet and the sink.
Raged about our budget and washed windows just to think.

He relished other women, the witch, the martyr and the saint
Bought magazines to ogle, studied Ruben's nudes in paint.

Soon he reaped his blindspot, not knowing what he'd sown
No mirror cast a light for him, he had no place called home

I walked away and chose, what was in my grasp, what's me.
And he watched but could not understand why I could not be he.

Save Me (Watercolor, 26 × 33)

Tennis, Anyone? (Watercolor, 14 × 20)

Mermaids (Watercolor, 28 × 35)

All-American Breakfast (Watercolor and collage, 28 × 35)

Going Up? (Watercolor, 28 × 35)

The Commuters (Watercolor and gouache, 36 × 28)

Emotions

The Aftermath (Watercolor, 22 × 30)

Emotions

Emotions drive the artist. Feelings push us and ask us to record them in our work. This intensity burns at the highest and lowest moments of life, providing fodder for the creative spirit. Things like injustice, pressure, love, loss, joy, anger, wonder, guilt, shame, loneliness, vulnerability, and grief are universal subjects; themes in life's drama.

Eulogies are examples of writing about life to write about death. They not only widen the perspective for others to remember the person who died, but are healing to those who compose them. We witness and testify when we put things down in concrete form; often what we choose to say is simple truth which inevitably is profound.

In our small town in Massachusetts, a boy who had been the youth leader at our church and a musical prodigy was killed by a sniper's bullet at his college. The grief over this tragedy was felt by the community in a way that is rarely expressed. At his memorial service the words people read to celebrate his life were funny, angry, loving, and thought-provoking. As I listened, I experienced a full range of emotions. Each writing was radically honest and fervent; alive.

An unforgettable image of that day were the friends of the boy's mother, who surrounded her and grieved with her. I wanted to write something about the injustice of this boy's death, but I couldn't; not until I abstractly drew the doodle I ultimately translated into a painting. In *The Aftermath* I used primary colors and a stained glass window effect to express the spirit that pervaded the church. Once my feelings were released in the painting, the poem, "The Statistic," came easily.

The Statistic

He was sixteen
a sage's soul sent to
write cantatas
and go barefoot to church
to drink life and
teach us
how to
laugh at ourselves
until we cried
for him

Word War

The mother and daughter fought,
No boundaries held them back,
They were war machines
Oiled with hurt
Fired with fossilized fuel.

Their tongues became scissors
Brains spinning like bobbins
Unraveling threads that had
Held them together
Over deserts and rivers
Canyons and clouds
Splitting them apart
To separate victories

Word War (Acrylic and Tempera, 22 × 34)

The Voyeur's Portrait

Freckled arms
at rest

An abandoned book
lost to a belly's eye

Face hidden
under umbrellas of shade

Legs stretched
toward the surf and

a gaggle of girls
too young
to remember
a beach that
once was his.

The Voyeur's Portrait (Watercolor, 20 × 14)

Trapped!

Let me out! Take down the walls
Crumble the concrete that's stacked
Between us—bring on a jackhammer
Let me dance to a wood nymph's tune
Not this solitary moan that climbs
Up the walls and down
That drowns out children playing.
Let me take on the wind
Rush to catch the last cricket
Before winter freezes the tall grass.

The Crunch (Watercolor, 22 × 30)

Mourning

The moon has fallen
eclipsed into the sea,
taking its silver and gold
to the very bottom
for the likes of starfish
and flatfaced flounders.

Those above
mourn lost light
and the
gilded pathways to somewhere.
No illumination now,
No dancing smiles of
ripples on the surface.
Only a broad dark expanse
Umber   silent   dense.

Starfish (Watercolor, 14 × 18)

Sunday Morning

I am layered in cotton and lamb's wool
Sprinting from the house.
My well-used bed behind me.
Panties caught in rumpled folds.
The frigid air
Pushes me to a warmed car,
Its door opened by loving hands,
Hands that know my secrets.
We do not need to talk.
We pass the familiar;
Star Market, Carlson Real Estate,
Gulf Gas, Royale Tire, the graveyard.
It's then I see him,
Kneeling before a stone.
Hair whipped flat against his temples
His hat in his hands, coat billowing
Black against gray sky.
I turned to Dennis just to say
Words that can't explain
A man in the morning
Mourning alone.

The Widower

Morning is always the hardest, Love.
Sundays are the worst,
The day to roll over and play,
No clocks ticking in our heads.
You know, I miss your bad coffee?
Haven't even opened the *Times*.
Remember how we'd make love,
Somewhere between Business Week
And Arts and Leisure?
You would examine my moles,
Worry about their color.
I'd bite your lips and you'd forget.
We'd stay in bed for hours
Eat doughnuts, sometimes,
After we reviewed the Book Reviews.

You'd insist I wash the newsprint off my hands
To protect us from lead poisoning.
You always worried so.
I should have worried more.
I never knew how your warm limbs
Made my life flow.
Your laughter gave me mine.
Your sex set me free.

I want to rip away this stone
I want to climb next to you
I have a secret I forgot to tell you.
I won't care if you cry.

A Woman and Her Rose (Watercolor, 16 × 20)

Wild Women

Wild women use red in their paintings
Scream a yellow hillside
Push pink into the night sky.

Wild women let lives tangle and
Watch as their words skip across pages
Leading to dark planets,
The other side of the moon.

Wild women put their Ph.D.s in chalices
Place them on the altar and run away
To play with color squares and magic markers.

Wild women cry when they remember
Laugh at all they know they know. . . .
Then dance like nymphs in the moonlight.

Women Who Unravel the Moon (Acrylic, 30 × 36)

Comet Hale-Bopp at Easter

From the mangers of space
The millennium has sent a messenger
To alert the comatose,
Announce a new age.

Apocalyptic floods and fires,
Quakes and avenging angels
Have flown before this surprise.

Stand still and listen
To the ancient roll of drums,
The wails of mastodons,
The silence of passenger pigeons
In the swish of its gossamer tails.

Ten thousand generations
Have come and gone in its wake.
Moses descended his hilltop,
Christ abandoned his tomb,
Quetzalcotl's plumes became legend.

But right now, in this twinkling moment,
This poetic pause,
We are given another chance
To pay attention, and wonder.

Awe for the Night Sky (Watercolor, 14 × 18)

Apology

To you brave ant, formidable formicidae,
      upon whose social order I wreak havoc
      drowning you in chemicals
      attempting to annihilate your legions
      even as I watched you carry off a brother
      larger than yourself:

To you pale grass who danced and tickled my shins,
      who bloomed the clover and fed the cow,
      who held the water and stop stopped the flood
      who thrived on wormy waste and canine shit
      only to be cut down by the severing
      steel of whirring blades:

To daisies everywhere
      whose roots were turned asunder
      held in hands like mine that
      plucked your petals one by one—
      asking if he loved me or loved me not
      left quivering in my wake:

To the weavers, the spinners,
      the ladies of lace who patiently spun
      despite the fright of Miss Muffet;
      whose arachnid art of silken traps,
      and fine repelling ropes was lost
      to my swift banishing broom;

To the crawlers
      the nesters
          the grazers
             the bloomers
                the burrowers
                    the swimmers
                        the climbers
I cannot be all I want to be to you and I am sorry.

Roadside Lace (Watercolor, 22 × 30)

Teaching America

Summer brought silence
To my Brooklyn street.
Those who could, left,
And everyone I knew, did.
I was only seven,
My father dead that spring,
My mother numb,
My best friend floating on a raft
Somewhere north of the city.

And then I found them,
A boy and a girl,
Sitting on their stoop,
Solemn and foreign;
The only other children left behind.
When I saw the numbers
Printed on their wrists,
I wanted to know where they'd gone,
But they covered themselves and wouldn't tell.

I had been stamped at the circus.

They tried to smile—
I remember that—
But they weren't as good at it as me
And they didn't know how to play.
I had no choice but to teach them,
Though all I knew was make-believe.

They tolerated me so well—
The cowboys and Indians,
Rose bushes for cactus,
Vestibules for caves,
Broom handle horses,
Good guys and bad—

I was teaching them America!
I shot them dead every day,
But they never shot me.
They never really learned how to play.

The Hobby Horse (Watercolor and ink, 14 × 18)

The Fire on the Lawn

What was she feeling, that young mother,
walking the long stretch from the railroad station,
one hand weighted with a tired suitcase,
the other gripping her daughter's slim hand?
Was she returning to her husband
for her God or her father's approval?

When did she see the smoking pyre
against the crisp whiteness of her house?
Recognize the smoldering strap of her satin slip,
the charred buttons of her Sunday dress, a buckle,
in the black heap centered on grass where
once upon a time dandelions had bloomed her salad?

Was she shielded from the neighbors'
stares as they watched her approach? Did she keep
her step steady, head high? What grace allowed her
to pass the curtained windows, face the shame
of rumored causes, the implosion of dignity?

Which was the greatest loss? The dried corsages,
her portfolio from art school,
the leather-bound Kristin Lavransdatter or
those pictures of her first love smiling from a camel's
hump? Did her catechism burn?

Surely it was not the hubris of Icarus
that moved her toward the cruelty,
toward the angular man in the doorway,
the husband Father Sheehan called a sacred trust,
past his sneering smile, the eyes meant to punish,
the hands that built such a fire.

How did she move through the alcoholic mist,
beyond his stinking breath; his malevolence,
past the chair, the table, the littered kitchen,
little Joanie, alongside, ignoring her calico room
with its ragdolls and pink blankets?

Did the young woman hide in the bathroom,
to fall silently to her knees behind a hollow door,
embrace the child, and hear her small voice say,
"Don't be afraid, Mommy, it was just a accident!"?

Gloucester Train Station (Watercolor, 12 × 16)

Dennis Sleeping

on your shoulder
a golden edge
defines the dormant
heap of you
who does not know
my stare
my search
my desires to climb inside
your folds

limp arms stretch
towards me
your knee hair tickles mine
my breath stops short
at my desire to pluck them
to wake you
and prevent the abyss
should you choose to leave
in the way station
between night and morning

I must tell you
you can never go
not even after
the alarm is turned off

we must batten down the windows
draw the dead bolt
lock ourselves in.

The Nap (Watercolor, 30 × 22)

Where Lilies Bloom (Oil, 11 × 14)

Myths, Dreams, and Shadow Play

A Little Night Music (Watercolor and gouache, 24 × 30)

Myths, Dreams, and Shadow Play

Myths tell us where things stem from: things like jealousy, love, and the rainbow, to name a few. These first stories provide a universal anthology for explaining the unknown. They are in all cultures and accepted with a kind of poetic grace. Myths belong to the family of fables, fairy tales, religion, philosophy, and science fiction. It is only natural that literary references and variations of mythic themes are inherent in art and literature today.

Dreams have a relationship to myth. Both teach through poetic imagery. Dream language is cloaked in symbols muted by sleep, where we can look at our subconscious and deal with wishes, needs, and fears. Witty, inventive, informative, and full of puns, dreams spring from a metaphoric well of information offered to us without our asking. It is in dreams that we can fly and fall great distances. It is in dreams we experience monsters and unspeakable terrors; we kiss movie stars and ride like jockeys on unicorns.

Myths and dreams live on the periphery of our awareness, like shadow play: not always distinct, but real enough to frame our experiences. Of course, shadows themselves have myriad roles. They are cool spots under trees, a threat on a nursery wall, or a relief in a rush of hot color. They can be a zone of neutrality, a resting spot, a hiding place. Their existence dignifies what is exposed, intensifies and celebrates it. In shadows, we imagine more than we can see. Painters lean on shadows to dramatize light.

Exercise

Read about Diana, the huntress and patron of women. Paint or write about her in a contemporary setting.

Shoe Stories

Look at the foot, my mother said,
to gauge the measure of a man.
His shoe reveals his character
and how he'll play his hand.

Cinderella's older sisters were
disdained and undone,
with feet as testimony
to a future of humdrum.

Poor Clementine was lost forever.
Her big feet, a mere size nine (!)
were wearing boxes without topses
when she faced the foaming brine.

When brave Dorothy left Oz
she clicked her ruby heels
And took off for sunny Kansas
Despite the Munchkins' squeals.

Red Shoes are meant for torture
in Anderson's famed tale.
The maid who donned these slippers
Danced on to no avail.

The taproots of foot fetishes
stem from mythology;
else what could be their rationale,
I mean, psychologically?

The Shoe Fetish (Oil, 20 × 10)

Iris's Account

On the first day I created pink
Placed it in a water lily, tinted a baby's buns
Let it kiss a young girl's cheek—
    I learned tenderness.

On the second day I imagined yellow,
Pulled it through the clouds, dappled a forest floor
Painted morning rooftops—
    I learned hope.

On the third day I wept blue
Splashed it in the garden, sent it out to sea
Watched it raise a canopy above my head—
    I learned perspective.

On the fourth day I saw red and
Felt its power fill my veins, bled on city streets
Made a bull go mad—
    I learned passion

On the fifth day I ordered purple
Paraded it through town and left it in a shadow.
Discovered elegance and mystery—
    I learned restraint

On the sixth day I called forth orange
Grabbed its heat to dapple fields and fish, then
Gave it to the evening sky, to butterflies and fruit—
    I learned altruism.

On the seventh day I played with green
Poured its fertile stream over my brain, my breasts, my hands
Became one with all things new and called myself Goddess—
    I learned joy.

Josephine's Gift (Watercolor, 18 × 24)

The Subway

Just us,
Cloistered in
A steel space,
Smelling
Imposed sweat,
Swinging in
Uncertain grace.

Diverted eyes
Search familiar ads
Of toothpaste and
Delinquent dads.

Subway Dreaming (Watercolor, ink, and collage, 26 × 35)

The Nightmare

I fall
into a well so deep no light
can find its way.
I am I driving a toy car.
My steering wheel is broken.
It's then I see them,
wearing rubber masks and
driving bumper cars.
From the shadows, they ambush me
in a game designed for torture.
I am the brunt of the dark joke
battered and squashed on all sides
by these adults in children's clothes;
strange outfits of fuscia, chartreuse, and electric blue.
Each face shines and reflects ghoulish intentions
A strange hilarity contorts their nonexistent lips
but I am not laughing.
I maintain my dignity.
I can pretend as well as they.

Masks (Watercolor and gouache, 24 × 35)

Revision

Don't tell me God is sitting on a throne
Don't tell me he is up when I am down
That he is he, when I am she
Don't tell me God is in the sword
The buzz saw, the M-16
No. No God of mine declares a war
Kills a river
Beats down that hungry child
Tramples dreams.

My God evokes the pen
The brush, the melody.
Her eyes open mine
To see leafcutters, Venus, a high mesa.
Her ears delight in rolling surf
The haunting cry of coyote
The rustle of leaves
The first cry of a newborn.
Her hands tremble at the touch of flesh
The magnitude of expectation.
Her knees wobble on mountain slopes
At the integrity of a sunset.
A child's pirouette.
With her feet rooted to the ground
She knows from she whence she came
And where she will return.

Flying with the Muse (Watercolor, 12 × 18)

Women Who Run from Wolves (Watercolor, 28 × 34)

Experiment: Art as Play

Experiment

Art is not about making concessions; it is about play.

—Pablo Picasso

When Picasso first distorted the female form, do you not think it was an amusing exercise? Mais, oui!

When Jackson Pollack first splashed around his paint do you think he was playing? Of course!

How about the first time those colorful bubbles on a pointillist's brush fell off its tip and rolled green, yellow, blue, and orange dots to make a daisy in the grass? Was that not fun?

Georgia O'Keefe dreamed of lines and loved watching them emerge on sheets of paper, like thoughts growing out of themselves.

Watch a child with a bucket of paint dip and dab and splash and not apologize. The experience approximates joy. Do the same.

Experiment

On common poster paper or manila paper, paint bold shapes in pure tempera colors, not letting your colors meet. Use a hair dryer or the sun to quicken the drying of your painting. Now, you must trust in magic and cover your painting with India ink. When you wash off the ink you will see a wonderful collaboration of you and the elements; but more importantly, if time has disappeared, you will have succeeded. You have been *playing* with paint!

Scarlet Sky (Tempera and ink, 14 × 20)

Reminder

Look to the morning glories.
Beyond formal pruning,
They drape themselves on picket fences,
Casually climb through crooked slats
And explore negative space.
On weathered posts and knotty wire
Snags only help them stretch
Towards one another and beyond.
They reach for the light,
Confident in what they are—nature's
Flowers, opening in a slant of sun.

Blue Fugue (Oil on paper, 24 × 16)

The Ride (Watercolor, 28 × 33)

Play

When we were small and played school, we were practicing. The same was true when we bathed our dolls, built forts, sold lemonade, dressed up and pretended to be back-up singers.

Our play was a rehearsal for what was to follow. It was a teaching tool we utilized as naturally as we did our legs to walk. No one ever told us that playtime had to end at eighteen, or at some age called *adult*, and yet too many of us are not sure about its role in "real" life. Remember the platitude, *all work and no play makes Johnny a dull boy?* Well, the same is true for Johnny when he becomes a man.

The play *must* go on. Without it we cannot grow, create, or enjoy life as it moves us forward. Play requires no analysis, no belaboring philosophical questions, but it's as important as breathing. It nurtures and pleases. It teaches us to lose and to win. It lets us experiment. Play is a matter of choice and invention, allowing us to make every day eventful.

Don't just stop to smell the roses; paint them, plant them, arrange them, reconstruct them, and write about them. Own the roses utilizing your divine ability to interpret, recreate, and record. When you do, life's dimensions will become so broad you won't remember the confinements of space or the restrictions of time. You will be playing with the only universe you can ever understand—your own.

So, just ask me, "Can Carol come out and play?"

And I'll say, "I hope so. I hope so, forever!"

The Wannabees (Watercolor, 27 × 35)